CHECKERBOARD BIOGRAPHY LIBRARY

U.S. PRESIDENTS

The
United States Presidents

GROVER CLEVELAND

ABDO Publishing Company

BreAnn Rumsch

visit us at
www.abdopublishing.com

Published by ABDO Publishing Company, 8000 West 78th Street, Edina, Minnesota 55439.
Copyright © 2009 by Abdo Consulting Group, Inc. International copyrights reserved in all
countries. No part of this book may be reproduced in any form without written permission from the
publisher. The Checkerboard Library™ is a trademark and logo of ABDO Publishing Company.

Printed in the United States.

Cover Photo: Getty Images
Interior Photos: Alamy pp. 9, 14–15; AP Images p. 29; Corbis pp. 17, 19, 22, 27; iStockphoto
    pp. 16, 32; Library of Congress pp. 5, 10, 21, 23, 24, 25; National Archives p. 20; National
    Portrait Gallery, Smithsonian Institution / Art Resource p. 13; Picture History pp. 8, 11, 28

Editor: Heidi M.D. Elston
Art Direction & Cover Design: Neil Klinepier
Interior Design: Neil Klinepier

Library of Congress Cataloging-in-Publication Data

Rumsch, BreAnn, 1981-
 Grover Cleveland / BreAnn Rumsch.
     p. cm. -- (The United States presidents)
 Includes index.
 ISBN 978-1-60453-446-7
 1. Cleveland, Grover, 1837-1908--Juvenile literature. 2. Presidents--United States--Biography--
Juvenile literature. I. Title.

 E697.R86 2009
 973.8'5092--dc22
 [B]

                        2008033510

CONTENTS

Grover Cleveland 4

Timeline 6

Did You Know? 7

Young Grover 8

New York Lawyer 10

The Veto Mayor 14

President Cleveland 18

An Early Retirement 22

Back in Office 26

After the White House 28

Office of the President 30

Presidents and Their Terms 34

Glossary 38

Web Sites 39

Index 40

GROVER CLEVELAND

Grover Cleveland served as the twenty-second and twenty-fourth president of the United States. Cleveland is the only president to serve two terms that were not in a row.

Before his presidency, Cleveland worked as a lawyer and a sheriff. He also served as mayor of Buffalo, New York. Then, he was elected governor of New York.

In 1884, Cleveland was elected president. He was the first **Democrat** elected in 28 years. As president, Cleveland fought for **tariff** reform and a strong money system.

Four years later, President Cleveland ran for reelection. However, he did not win. He and his wife moved to New York City, New York. For the next four years, Cleveland worked there as a lawyer. He also remained interested in politics.

In 1892, Cleveland was elected president for a second time. Soon after, a **depression** began. President Cleveland tried to end it, but his attempts were unsuccessful. When his second term ended, Cleveland retired to Princeton, New Jersey.

4

As president, Cleveland's leadership was not always popular. But, he did what he believed was right for his country. Eventually, Americans came to respect his ideas and his honesty.

Grover Cleveland

TIMELINE

1837 - On March 18, Stephen Grover Cleveland was born in Caldwell, New Jersey.

1856 - Cleveland worked on Democrat James Buchanan's presidential campaign.

1862 - In New York, Cleveland was elected supervisor of Buffalo's Second Ward.

1863 - Cleveland became assistant district attorney of Erie County, New York.

1870 - Cleveland was elected sheriff of Erie County, where he served until 1873.

1881 - Cleveland was elected mayor of Buffalo, where he became known as the Veto Mayor.

1883 - On January 3, Cleveland became governor of New York.

1885 - On March 4, Cleveland became the twenty-second U.S. president.

1886 - In January, Cleveland asked Congress to pass the Presidential Succession Act; on June 2, Cleveland married Frances Folsom.

1887 - Cleveland signed the Dawes General Allotment Act in February; he signed the Interstate Commerce Act.

1888 - Cleveland lost reelection.

1891 - Cleveland spoke out against the Sherman Silver Purchase Act.

1893 - On March 4, Cleveland became the twenty-fourth U.S. president; a depression began in May.

1894 - Cleveland sent troops to Chicago, Illinois, to stop the Pullman strike.

1897 - Cleveland retired to Princeton, New Jersey.

1908 - Grover Cleveland died on June 24.

DID YOU KNOW?

Esther Cleveland was the first and only president's child born in the White House.

Many people think the Baby Ruth candy bar was named for famous baseball player Babe Ruth. However, others claim it was named after President Cleveland's daughter Ruth. When she was born, many Americans called her "Baby Ruth."

During Cleveland's second term, he developed cancer in his mouth. Cleveland did not want Americans to worry about his illness. So, his doctors secretly performed surgery aboard a boat in New York Harbor.

The Statue of Liberty was a gift from France to the United States. Cleveland advised Congress to accept the gift. He also dedicated the statue during a ceremony on October 28, 1886.

PRESIDENT OF THE
POTUS
UNITED STATES

YOUNG GROVER

Stephen Grover Cleveland was born in Caldwell, New Jersey, on March 18, 1837. Starting at a young age, everyone called him Grover.

Grover's parents were Richard and Ann Cleveland. Richard was a Presbyterian minister. The Cleveland family was large. Grover had three brothers and five sisters. He was the fifth child.

In 1841, Grover and his family moved to Fayetteville, New York. There, he attended Fayetteville Academy. Grover studied hard, but he was not the best student. In his free time, Grover liked to fish and hunt.

Ann Cleveland

FAST FACTS

BORN - March 18, 1837
WIFE - Frances Folsom
          (1864–1947)
CHILDREN - 5
POLITICAL PARTY - Democrat
AGE AT INAUGURATIONS - 47, 55
YEARS SERVED - 1885–1889, 1893–1897
VICE PRESIDENTS - Thomas A. Hendricks,
                    Adlai E. Stevenson
DIED - June 24, 1908, age 71

8

When Grover was 14, his family moved to Clinton, New York. There, Grover attended school for one term. Then from 1852 to 1853, he

Grover's birthplace in Caldwell, New Jersey

worked as a clerk in a general store. Grover earned money to help his father support the family.

By 1853, Grover's father was in poor health. So, he moved the family to Holland Patent, New York. There, he took an easier job. Shortly after arriving, Richard Cleveland died. Now Grover needed to help support his family.

Grover accepted a teaching position at the New York Institution for the Blind. His older brother, William, was also a teacher there. Grover worked at the school for one year.

NEW YORK LAWYER

In 1854, Cleveland decided to move west. He and a friend set off toward Cleveland, Ohio. On the way, they stopped in Buffalo, New York.

There, Cleveland visited his uncle Lewis F. Allen. Allen convinced him to stay in Buffalo. Allen helped his nephew get a job as a clerk in a law office. Cleveland learned as much as he could about law. He read many law books and observed lawyers at work.

In Buffalo, Cleveland soon became interested in politics. He began his political career in 1856 by working on **Democrat** James Buchanan's presidential campaign. Buchanan won the election. From then on, Cleveland would associate himself with the Democratic Party.

James Buchanan was president of the United States from 1857 to 1861.

In Buffalo, Cleveland worked at the law office of Rogers, Bowen, and Rogers. There, he earned four dollars a week.

Cleveland passed the examination to become a lawyer in 1859. He continued working for the same law firm as a clerk. Soon, he was promoted to chief clerk.

In 1862, Cleveland was elected supervisor of Buffalo's Second Ward. Then in 1863, he became assistant **district attorney** of Erie County, New York. Cleveland was successful at his job. Some days, he won all of his cases!

Meanwhile, the American **Civil War** was being fought. The United States needed more soldiers. So government officials passed a **conscription** law. In May 1863, Cleveland was selected to serve in the war. However, he was supporting his mother and sisters. So, Cleveland hired someone to go to war in his place.

In 1865, Cleveland ran for Erie County district attorney. However, he lost the election. So, Cleveland found work as a lawyer.

Then in 1870, Cleveland was elected sheriff of Erie County. As sheriff, Cleveland worked well with lawyers. He kept the jail running smoothly and served **warrants** promptly. Cleveland's term as sheriff ended in 1873. For the next eight years, he practiced law in Buffalo.

Cleveland was a hardworking assistant district attorney. After attending court all day, he would often work in his office until three o'clock in the morning.

THE VETO MAYOR

In 1881, **Democrats** nominated Cleveland to run for mayor of Buffalo. His opponent was **Republican** Milton C. Beebe. Cleveland won the election! As mayor, he **vetoed** many dishonest bills. Cleveland became known as the Veto Mayor.

The city council wanted Cleveland to approve a street-cleaning contract in 1882. However, council members had tried to **defraud** the city government of money. So Cleveland vetoed the bill. He told the council members to hire a company with a fair price.

Cleveland's honest reputation grew. That year, Democrats nominated him for governor of New York. He easily won the election.

Cleveland took office on January 3, 1883. As governor, he maintained his honest approach to work. Cleveland did not grant special favors or make secret deals. In fact, he conducted business with his office door left open. People often visited him while he worked.

Outside Buffalo City Hall stands a bronze statue in honor of Cleveland.

As governor, Cleveland continued to **veto** dishonest bills. And, he supported reform bills. He passed laws that required bank inspections, prison reforms, and protection for the rights of voters. Cleveland also signed a bill to preserve the land around Niagara Falls in New York. This land later became a state park.

Niagara Falls State Park is the oldest state park in the United States.

The **Democratic** Party had high hopes for Cleveland. In 1884, Democrats nominated Cleveland for president. They chose Thomas A. Hendricks as his **running mate**. The **Republicans** nominated James G. Blaine for president. Illinois senator John A. Logan became his running mate.

Many Republicans distrusted Blaine. They refused to support him. Instead, they voted for Cleveland. These Republicans became known as mugwumps.

It was a very close election. There was no clear winner at first. After three days of recounting votes, Cleveland was declared the winner. He won by fewer than 25,000 **popular votes**.

James G. Blaine

PRESIDENT CLEVELAND

On March 4, 1885, Cleveland took office. His first task was to name his **cabinet** and fill **civil service** jobs. New presidents usually fill these positions with people from their own political party. This is called the spoils system.

Cleveland was the first **Democratic** president in 28 years. So, **Republicans** held most of the civil service jobs. They did not want to be replaced by Democrats.

Republicans reminded President Cleveland about the Tenure of Office Act. It said the president could not remove people from office without U.S. Senate approval. But Cleveland felt the president did not have to answer to the Senate. This is called executive privilege.

President Cleveland did not agree with the spoils system. So he filled the positions with qualified people, whether they were

SUPREME
COURT
APPOINTMENTS

LUCIUS Q.C. LAMAR - 1888
MELVILLE WESTON FULLER - 1888

18

President Cleveland's first inauguration took place at the U.S. Capitol in Washington, D.C.

Democrats or not. Then, Cleveland worked to **repeal** the Tenure of Office Act. Congress repealed it two years later.

When Cleveland took office, U.S. currency was an important issue. President Cleveland supported the gold standard. This system allowed money to be exchanged for a fixed amount of gold.

However, the Bland-Allison Act had been passed in 1878. It allowed money to be made from silver as well as gold. The act also required the U.S. **Treasury** to buy silver for coining into money.

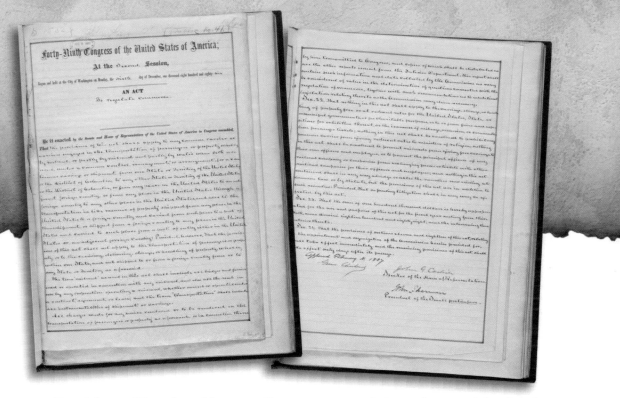

President Cleveland knew silver was worth less than gold. So, he believed the Bland-Allison Act threatened the U.S. **economy**. Cleveland asked Congress to **repeal** the Bland-Allison Act. However, Congress refused.

Meanwhile, Vice President Hendricks had died on November 25, 1885. Cleveland worried about who would be president if he died as well. So in January 1886, he asked Congress to approve the

Mr. and Mrs. Cleveland

Presidential Succession Act. This act specified who would lead the country if the president and vice president could not.

That same year, Cleveland married Frances Folsom on June 2. Cleveland was the first president to get married in the White House.

In February 1887, President Cleveland signed the Dawes General Allotment Act. This act gave land and U.S. citizenship to Native Americans. But first, they had to give up their **reservation** land. Cleveland also signed the Interstate Commerce Act that year. This allowed the government to manage railroads that traveled through different states.

By the end of 1887, the U.S. **Treasury** had a large **surplus**. Cleveland believed the nation's high **tariffs** had caused the surplus. So, he asked Congress to lower tariffs. He thought this would improve the **economy**. The lower prices would help Americans, too.

AN EARLY RETIREMENT

The year 1888 was an election year. **Democrats** liked Cleveland's policies, so they renominated him for president. Allen G. Thurman was named his **running mate**. The **Republicans** nominated Benjamin Harrison. Levi P. Morton became his running mate.

The election of 1888 was one of the most unusual in U.S. history. President Cleveland won about 100,000 more **popular votes** than Harrison. However, Harrison had 233 electoral votes to Cleveland's 168. So Harrison won the election.

The tariff issue was central to the 1888 election. Cleveland wanted to lower tariffs, while Harrison opposed tariff reduction.

In March 1889, the Clevelands left the White House and moved to New York City. Cleveland worked there as a lawyer. In 1891, the Clevelands had their first child. They named their daughter Ruth. The Clevelands went on to have four more children. They were named Esther, Marion, Richard, and Francis.

Americans rejoiced at the birth of Cleveland's first child, Ruth.

Adlai E. Stevenson

Congress had passed the Sherman Silver Purchase Act in 1890. It increased the amount of silver the government purchased each month. Cleveland still believed the gold standard system was better for the **economy**. So in February 1891, he spoke out against the act.

Some **Democrats** disagreed with Cleveland's support of the gold standard. Yet, Cleveland was renominated for president in 1892. This time, Adlai E. Stevenson became his **running mate**. The **Republicans** renominated President Harrison. They chose Whitelaw Reid as his running mate.

During the campaign, a strike took place in Homestead, Pennsylvania. President Harrison sent troops there to stop it. His actions angered many Americans. So, Cleveland easily won the election. He received 277 electoral votes to Harrison's 145.

Benjamin Harrison was president of the United States from 1889 to 1893.

BACK IN OFFICE

Cleveland began his second term on March 4, 1893. Earlier that year, a small group of Americans had seized control of the Hawaiian Islands. They wanted the United States to **annex** the islands. However, Cleveland believed Hawaii had been overthrown unfairly. So he stopped Congress from annexing Hawaii.

In May 1893, a **depression** began. President Cleveland blamed the Sherman Silver Purchase Act passed during Harrison's term. He worked with Congress to **repeal** the act.

Meanwhile, the nation's gold supplies had dropped. President Cleveland asked bankers to sell government **bonds** to other countries. The bankers received gold in exchange. This renewed U.S. gold supplies. Yet, the depression continued.

Americans began to revolt. The worst strike happened in Chicago, Illinois, in 1894. Workers at the Pullman Palace Car Company felt their wages had been cut unfairly. Due to the strike, the U.S. mail could not be delivered. So, President Cleveland sent troops to Chicago to stop the strike. Businesses were happy, but many workers were not.

PRESIDENT CLEVELAND'S CABINET

FIRST TERM
MARCH 4, 1885– MARCH 4, 1889

- **STATE** – Thomas F. Bayard
- **TREASURY** – Daniel Manning
  Charles S. Fairchild (from April 1, 1887)
- **WAR** – William C. Endicott
- **NAVY** – William C. Whitney
- **ATTORNEY GENERAL** – Augustus H. Garland
- **INTERIOR** – Lucius Q.C. Lamar
  William F. Vilas (from January 16, 1888)
- **AGRICULTURE** – Norman J. Colman
  (from February 3, 1889)

SECOND TERM
MARCH 4, 1893– MARCH 4, 1897

- **STATE** – Walter Q. Gresham
  Richard Olney (from June 10, 1895)
- **TREASURY** – John G. Carlisle
- **WAR** – Daniel S. Lamont
- **NAVY** – Hilary A. Herbert
- **ATTORNEY GENERAL** – Richard Olney
  Judson Harmon (from June 11, 1895)
- **INTERIOR** – Hoke Smith
  David R. Francis (from September 4, 1896)
- **AGRICULTURE** – J. Sterling Morton

Cleveland (center)
with his second
cabinet in 1897

AFTER THE WHITE HOUSE

By 1896, many **Democrats** no longer agreed with Cleveland's support of the gold standard. They were ready for a new candidate.

Cleveland at Westland in Princeton, New Jersey

Cleveland was also ready to retire. So, he and his family left the White House in March 1897. They moved to Princeton, New Jersey. There, they settled in a home they called Westland.

Cleveland soon became active at Princeton University. In 1901, he became a Princeton **trustee**. He also gave speeches at the school and wrote articles. Yet, Cleveland was never too busy to go hunting and fishing.

Cleveland also enjoyed spending time with his family. Sadly, Ruth died suddenly in 1904. The entire Cleveland family was heartbroken.

After Ruth's death, Cleveland continued to write and give speeches. Eventually, his health grew poor. He suffered from heart trouble.

Cleveland is buried in the old Princeton Cemetery. His wife was buried beside him after her death in 1947.

Grover Cleveland died on June 24, 1908. His last words were, "I have tried so hard to do right."

Grover Cleveland brought honesty and honor to all of his public offices. As president, he fought for the gold standard. He also led the country through a **depression**. Some of Cleveland's beliefs made him unpopular. However, he always stood up for what he thought was right.

OFFICE OF THE PRESIDENT

BRANCHES OF GOVERNMENT

The U.S. government is divided into three branches. They are the executive, legislative, and judicial branches. This division is called a separation of powers. Each branch has some power over the others. This is called a system of checks and balances.

EXECUTIVE BRANCH

The executive branch enforces laws. It is made up of the president, the vice president, and the president's cabinet. The president represents the United States around the world. He or she oversees relations with other countries and signs treaties. The president signs bills into law and appoints officials and federal judges. He or she also leads the military and manages government workers.

LEGISLATIVE BRANCH

The legislative branch makes laws, maintains the military, and regulates trade. It also has the power to declare war. This branch consists of the Senate and the House of Representatives. Together, these two houses make up Congress. Each state has two senators. A state's population determines the number of representatives it has.

JUDICIAL BRANCH

The judicial branch interprets laws. It consists of district courts, courts of appeals, and the Supreme Court. District courts try cases. If a person disagrees with a trial's outcome, he or she may appeal. If the courts of appeals support the ruling, a person may appeal to the Supreme Court. The Supreme Court also makes sure that laws follow the U.S. Constitution.

QUALIFICATIONS FOR OFFICE

To be president, a person must meet three requirements. A candidate must be at least 35 years old and a natural-born U.S. citizen. He or she must also have lived in the United States for at least 14 years.

ELECTORAL COLLEGE

The U.S. presidential election is an indirect election. Voters from each state choose electors to represent them in the Electoral College. The number of electors from each state is based on population. Each elector has one electoral vote. Electors are pledged to cast their vote for the candidate who receives the highest number of popular votes in their state. A candidate must receive the majority of Electoral College votes to win.

TERM OF OFFICE

Each president may be elected to two four-year terms. Sometimes, a president may only be elected once. This happens if he or she served more than two years of the previous president's term.

The presidential election is held on the Tuesday after the first Monday in November. The president is sworn in on January 20 of the following year. At that time, he or she takes the oath of office:

I do solemnly swear (or affirm) that I will faithfully execute the office of President of the United States, and will to the best of my ability, preserve, protect and defend the Constitution of the United States.

LINE OF SUCCESSION

The Presidential Succession Act of 1947 defines who becomes president if the president cannot serve. The vice president is first in the line of succession. Next are the Speaker of the House and the President Pro Tempore of the Senate. If none of these individuals is able to serve, the office falls to the president's cabinet members. They would take office in the order in which each department was created:

Secretary of State

Secretary of the Treasury

Secretary of Defense

Attorney General

Secretary of the Interior

Secretary of Agriculture

Secretary of Commerce

Secretary of Labor

Secretary of Health and Human Services

Secretary of Housing and Urban Development

Secretary of Transportation

Secretary of Energy

Secretary of Education

Secretary of Veterans Affairs

Secretary of Homeland Security

BENEFITS

• While in office, the president receives a salary of $400,000 each year. He or she lives in the White House and has 24-hour Secret Service protection.

• The president may travel on a Boeing 747 jet called Air Force One. The airplane can accommodate 70 passengers. It has kitchens, a dining room, sleeping areas, and a conference room. It also has fully equipped offices with the latest communications systems. Air Force One can fly halfway around the world before needing to refuel. It can even refuel in flight!

• If the president wishes to travel by car, he or she uses Cadillac One. Cadillac One is a Cadillac Deville. It has been modified with heavy armor and communications systems. The president takes Cadillac One along when visiting other countries if secure transportation will be needed.

• The president also travels on a helicopter called Marine One. Like the presidential car, Marine One accompanies the president when traveling abroad if necessary.

• Sometimes, the president needs to get away and relax with family and friends. Camp David is the official presidential retreat. It is located in the cool, wooded mountains in Maryland. The U.S. Navy maintains the retreat, and the U.S. Marine Corps keeps it secure. The camp offers swimming, tennis, golf, and hiking.

• When the president leaves office, he or she receives Secret Service protection for ten more years. He or she also receives a yearly pension of $191,300 and funding for office space, supplies, and staff.

PRESIDENTS AND THEIR TERMS

PRESIDENT	PARTY	TOOK OFFICE	LEFT OFFICE	TERMS SERVED	VICE PRESIDENT
George Washington	None	April 30, 1789	March 4, 1797	Two	John Adams
John Adams	Federalist	March 4, 1797	March 4, 1801	One	Thomas Jefferson
Thomas Jefferson	Democratic-Republican	March 4, 1801	March 4, 1809	Two	Aaron Burr, George Clinton
James Madison	Democratic-Republican	March 4, 1809	March 4, 1817	Two	George Clinton, Elbridge Gerry
James Monroe	Democratic-Republican	March 4, 1817	March 4, 1825	Two	Daniel D. Tompkins
John Quincy Adams	Democratic-Republican	March 4, 1825	March 4, 1829	One	John C. Calhoun
Andrew Jackson	Democrat	March 4, 1829	March 4, 1837	Two	John C. Calhoun, Martin Van Buren
Martin Van Buren	Democrat	March 4, 1837	March 4, 1841	One	Richard M. Johnson
William H. Harrison	Whig	March 4, 1841	April 4, 1841	Died During First Term	John Tyler
John Tyler	Whig	April 6, 1841	March 4, 1845	Completed Harrison's Term	Office Vacant
James K. Polk	Democrat	March 4, 1845	March 4, 1849	One	George M. Dallas
Zachary Taylor	Whig	March 5, 1849	July 9, 1850	Died During First Term	Millard Fillmore

PRESIDENT	PARTY	TOOK OFFICE	LEFT OFFICE	TERMS SERVED	VICE PRESIDENT
Millard Fillmore	Whig	July 10, 1850	March 4, 1853	Completed Taylor's Term	Office Vacant
Franklin Pierce	Democrat	March 4, 1853	March 4, 1857	One	William R.D. King
James Buchanan	Democrat	March 4, 1857	March 4, 1861	One	John C. Breckinridge
Abraham Lincoln	Republican	March 4, 1861	April 15, 1865	Served One Term, Died During Second Term	Hannibal Hamlin, Andrew Johnson
Andrew Johnson	Democrat	April 15, 1865	March 4, 1869	Completed Lincoln's Second Term	Office Vacant
Ulysses S. Grant	Republican	March 4, 1869	March 4, 1877	Two	Schuyler Colfax, Henry Wilson
Rutherford B. Hayes	Republican	March 3, 1877	March 4, 1881	One	William A. Wheeler
James A. Garfield	Republican	March 4, 1881	September 19, 1881	Died During First Term	Chester Arthur
Chester Arthur	Republican	September 20, 1881	March 4, 1885	Completed Garfield's Term	Office Vacant
Grover Cleveland	Democrat	March 4, 1885	March 4, 1889	One	Thomas A. Hendricks
Benjamin Harrison	Republican	March 4, 1889	March 4, 1893	One	Levi P. Morton
Grover Cleveland	Democrat	March 4, 1893	March 4, 1897	One	Adlai E. Stevenson
William McKinley	Republican	March 4, 1897	September 14, 1901	Served One Term, Died During Second Term	Garret A. Hobart, Theodore Roosevelt

PRESIDENTS 13–25, 1850–1901

PRESIDENT	PARTY	TOOK OFFICE	LEFT OFFICE	TERMS SERVED	VICE PRESIDENT
Theodore Roosevelt	Republican	September 14, 1901	March 4, 1909	Completed McKinley's Second Term, Served One Term	Office Vacant, Charles Fairbanks
William Taft	Republican	March 4, 1909	March 4, 1913	One	James S. Sherman
Woodrow Wilson	Democrat	March 4, 1913	March 4, 1921	Two	Thomas R. Marshall
Warren G. Harding	Republican	March 4, 1921	August 2, 1923	Died During First Term	Calvin Coolidge
Calvin Coolidge	Republican	August 3, 1923	March 4, 1929	Completed Harding's Term, Served One Term	Office Vacant, Charles Dawes
Herbert Hoover	Republican	March 4, 1929	March 4, 1933	One	Charles Curtis
Franklin D. Roosevelt	Democrat	March 4, 1933	April 12, 1945	Served Three Terms, Died During Fourth Term	John Nance Garner, Henry A. Wallace, Harry S. Truman
Harry S. Truman	Democrat	April 12, 1945	January 20, 1953	Completed Roosevelt's Fourth Term, Served One Term	Office Vacant, Alben Barkley
Dwight D. Eisenhower	Republican	January 20, 1953	January 20, 1961	Two	Richard Nixon
John F. Kennedy	Democrat	January 20, 1961	November 22, 1963	Died During First Term	Lyndon B. Johnson
Lyndon B. Johnson	Democrat	November 22, 1963	January 20, 1969	Completed Kennedy's Term, Served One Term	Office Vacant, Hubert H. Humphrey
Richard Nixon	Republican	January 20, 1969	August 9, 1974	Completed First Term, Resigned During Second Term	Spiro T. Agnew, Gerald Ford

PRESIDENT	PARTY	TOOK OFFICE	LEFT OFFICE	TERMS SERVED	VICE PRESIDENT
Gerald Ford	Republican	August 9, 1974	January 20, 1977	Completed Nixon's Second Term	Nelson A. Rockefeller
Jimmy Carter	Democrat	January 20, 1977	January 20, 1981	One	Walter Mondale
Ronald Reagan	Republican	January 20, 1981	January 20, 1989	Two	George H.W. Bush
George H.W. Bush	Republican	January 20, 1989	January 20, 1993	One	Dan Quayle
Bill Clinton	Democrat	January 20, 1993	January 20, 2001	Two	Al Gore
George W. Bush	Republican	January 20, 2001	January 20, 2009	Two	Dick Cheney
Barack Obama	Democrat	January 20, 2009			Joe Biden

"I have only one thing to do and that is to do right, and that is easy." Grover Cleveland

WRITE TO THE PRESIDENT

You may write to the president at:

The White House
1600 Pennsylvania Avenue NW
Washington, DC 20500

You may e-mail the president at:
comments@whitehouse.gov

GLOSSARY

annex - to take land and add it to a nation.

bond - a certificate sold by a government. The certificate promises to pay its purchase price plus interest on or after a given future date.

cabinet - a group of advisers chosen by the president to lead government departments.

civil service - the part of the government that is responsible for matters not covered by the military, the courts, or the law.

civil war - a war between groups in the same country. The United States of America and the Confederate States of America fought a civil war from 1861 to 1865.

conscription - forced enrollment by law in a country's armed forces.

defraud - to take something away from someone by trickery or deception.

Democrat - a member of the Democratic political party. When Grover Cleveland was president, Democrats supported farmers and landowners.

depression - a period of economic trouble when there is little buying or selling and many people are out of work.

district attorney - a lawyer for the government who works in a specific district, such as a county or a state.

economy - the way a nation uses its money, goods, and natural resources.

popular vote - the vote of the entire body of people with the right to vote.

repeal - to formally withdraw or cancel.

Republican - a member of the Republican political party. When Grover
  Cleveland was president, Republicans supported business and strong
  government.
reservation - a piece of land set aside by the government for Native Americans
  to live on.
running mate - a candidate running for a lower-rank position on an election
  ticket, especially the candidate for vice president.
surplus - an amount above what is needed.
tariff - the taxes a government puts on imported or exported goods.
treasury - a place where money is kept.
trustee - a person in charge of another person's or an organization's property or
  affairs.
veto - the right of one member of a decision-making group to stop an action
  by the group. In the U.S. government, the president can veto bills passed
  by Congress. But Congress can override the president's veto if two-thirds
  of its members vote to do so.
warrant - a document giving authority to an officer to make an arrest or
  conduct a search.

WEB SITES

To learn more about Grover Cleveland, visit ABDO Publishing Company on
the World Wide Web at **www.abdopublishing.com**. Web sites about Grover
Cleveland are featured on our Book Links page. These links are routinely
monitored and updated to provide the most current information available.

INDEX

A

American Civil War 12

B

Beebe, Milton C. 14
birth 8
Blaine, James G. 17
Bland-Allison Act 19, 20
Buchanan, James 10

C

childhood 8, 9

D

Dawes General Allotment
    Act 21
death 29
Democratic Party 4, 10, 14,
    17, 18, 19, 22, 24, 28
depression 4, 26, 29

E

education 8, 9, 10

F

family 4, 8, 9, 10, 12, 21,
    23, 28, 29

G

gold standard 19, 24, 28, 29
governor 4, 14, 16

H

Harrison, Benjamin 22, 24,
    25, 26
Hawaiian Islands 26
health 29
Hendricks, Thomas A. 17,
    20
Homestead Strike 25

I

inauguration 18, 26
Interstate Commerce Act 21

L

Logan, John A. 17

M

mayor 4, 14
Morton, Levi P. 22
mugwumps 17

N

Native Americans 21
Niagara Falls 16

P

Presidential Succession Act
    21
Princeton University 28
Pullman Strike 26

R

Reid, Whitelaw 24
religion 8
Republican Party 14, 17,
    18, 22, 24
retirement 4, 28, 29

S

sheriff 4, 12
Sherman Silver Purchase
    Act 24, 26
spoils system 18
Stevenson, Adlai E. 24

T

Tenure of Office Act 18, 19
Thurman, Allen G. 22
Treasury, U.S. 19, 21

W

Westland 28